Disney

BIG HERO 6

ビッグ・ヒーロー6

THE ESSENTIAL GUIDE

Disney
BIG HERO 6

THE ESSENTIAL GUIDE
Written by Glenn Dakin

Contents

Introduction

Welcome to San Fransokyo! In this gadget-crazy city there's one boy whose offbeat genius towers above the rest – it's just that nobody has noticed it yet. Hiro Hamada is a 14-year-old robotics whizz who could change the world... if he ever stops messing around.

It's lucky Hiro has some of the coolest super-nerd friends in the world. Honey, Wasabi and Go Go are all bright sparks at San Fransokyo Institute of Technology, the school Hiro dreams of going to. And then there's Fred. The less said about him the better.

One day, all Hiro's dreams of greatness may come true. But first he's going to face a massive challenge, a sinister foe and a mystery that takes him far beyond the streets he loves so much. Oh, and he's going to end up friends with a giant robot along the way. Step into Hiro's world and let the big hero action begin!

San Fransokyo

Glittering skyscrapers soar above the crowded streets and shadowy back alleys of this city that combines old and new in endless exciting ways. In San Fransokyo, science and technology are everywhere, and anyone with creativity and determination can rise up to become a hero.

Neon signs are in multiple languages

24-hour animated billboards

Where East meets West
Asian-influenced architecture and ramshackle noodle-bars sit side by side with hot dog stands and stately skyscrapers. The unique fusion flavour of this metropolis makes it an exciting place to be.

DID YOU KNOW?
San Fransokyo is built to withstand earthquakes, and its buildings are designed to survive swaying and shaking.

City of invention

Animated neon signs dazzle the eyes, colourful vending machines squeeze into every corner, and wind turbines fill the air like hovering zeppelins. San Fransokyo is a city of invention, where crime lords are more likely to have a bot fight than a gang war.

Aerial turbines produce power from the wind

Skybridges connect soaring towers

Jewel of the Pacific

A thriving city by the bay, San Fransokyo is a glittering jewel on the Pacific Rim. A multicultural metropolis, it is an example of a world where East meets West. Art and technology blend beautifully in this prosperous city.

Public transport tram system

Hiro

Meet Hiro Hamada! He may just be the brainiest kid in San Fransokyo, although don't tell him that. Inventive Hiro is crazy about building robots and is an expert in battle bots. Someday his genius could help the world – if he ever decides to break free of the battle bot fighting circuit.

Big brother knows best

Hiro's big brother Tadashi has always been there for him. He encourages Hiro's ideas – no matter how crazy – and tries to keep him out of trouble!

Nimble fingers for fine tech-work

Battle bot king

Two bots enter – one bot leaves! Hiro knows all there is to know about street bot fighting. When he takes on Mr Yama, the local champ, the battle lasts only seconds... and Hiro is the winner!

"IF I DON'T GO TO THIS NERD SCHOOL, I'M GOING TO LOSE MY MIND."

Cool hair should never look combed

T-shirt reveals love of armoured warrior bots

Comfortable and cool hoodie to wear at bot fights

Hiro's hideaway
In addition to his garage workshop, this bedroom is where Hiro has some of his best ideas. The shelves show how his love of robot toys evolved into him building his own creations.

Nerd heaven
Hiro thinks university is just a place where they tell you stuff you already know – until Tadashi takes him to his lab at San Fransokyo Tech. There Hiro meets his own hero, Professor Callaghan, author of "Callaghan's Law of Robotics". Suddenly university is the one place Hiro wants to be.

DID YOU KNOW?
Hiro's battle robot, "Megabot", has an edge – it is held together magnetically, so it can reassemble itself!

Tadashi

Kind, thoughtful and always dependable, Tadashi is the best big brother Hiro can imagine. He always gives Hiro sensible advice, and whenever Hiro doesn't take it – which is most days – big bro is still there to get him out of trouble.

DID YOU KNOW?

Tadashi has sewn mini GPS systems into every one of Hiro's hoodies, so he can keep tabs on his little brother.

Three's company

Three is the magic number for Tadashi's close-knit family unit. Aunt Cass looks after her nephews and they bring fun into her life.

School of hard knocks

Despite their caring relationship, the boys still love to fight and score points off each other. Martial arts bouts remind Hiro that Tadashi is still the boss!

Favourite
baseball cap

Fearless friend
Tadashi's super-sensible exterior hides a brave heart. He will always help out anyone in danger, no matter what the cost to himself.

Stylish yet
casual jacket

"I'M NOT GIVING UP ON YOU."

Changing the world
Don't let that relaxed look fool you – Tadashi is a tough, determined character who works all hours to perfect his "Baymax" personal healthcare companion. He feels passionately that science should free people from suffering and all his energy is invested in his project. More than anything, Tadashi wants Baymax to help a lot of people.

Man-bag for
gadgets and
research notes

Aunt Cass

Family comes first for Hiro's aunt, who has raised him and his brother ever since they were small. From her beloved café she keeps an eye on their comings and goings, and is sure to keep her customers up to speed with all their achievements.

The Lucky Cat Café

A hardworking, talented chef, Cass has built up a great little reputation for her café. Cass is business-savvy, too – she organises special events to drum up new customers.

DID YOU KNOW?

Cass has a soft spot for poetry, and often runs evening poetry readings at the café.

Meet Mochi

Cass's cat, Mochi, loves the attention he gets from the café customers. Things can go a little too far though, when Hiro and Tadashi invent new things for Mochi to try out!

Wild hair is Cass's trademark

Turquoise gemstone symbolises wisdom

Black t-shirt hides coffee stains

"I LOVE MY FAMILY."

Aunt in a million

The one thing that makes Cass burst with pride are the achievements of her boys. Her big dream is to see them studying at university together.

Secret of success

Aunt Cass provides Hiro and Tadashi with garage space to turn into a lab, feeds them brain-nurturing food and listens to their problems. She keeps everyone together, and is the boys' biggest supporter.

The Lucky Cat Café

Aunt Cass's café is her pride and joy and is a cool, cosy hangout for young and old. It is named after the traditional lucky cat ornament – or "beckoning cat" as it is sometimes called – with its right paw raised to bring good fortune.

Home-from-home
The café is like a second home for Hiro and his friends, who can always drop in for a warm welcome or even a shoulder to cry on. It also has many other regulars, like Mrs Matsuda, an 80-year-old who likes to wear age-inappropriate clothing.

Door to apartment upstairs

Table for two, for friendly chats

Aunt Cass's menu
Cass mixes a healthy approach – selling smoothies and fruit teas – with a love of treats. One of her specials is *Yakisoba-pan*, a chow mein hot dog.

San Fransokyo Tech

Every science student in the city dreams of winning a place at San Fransokyo Institute of Technology (SFIT). Whilst its futuristic architecture catches the eye, the rest of the campus was actually created over 100 years ago. Beautiful landscaped gardens contain peaceful lakes with traditional Japanese-style footbridges.

Round windows enhance flowing design

Flower gardens create tranquil environment

Professor Callaghan

Robotics Professor Robert Callaghan is a legend at SFIT, and famous around the world as the inventor of "Callaghan's Law of Robotics". He demands 100% commitment from his students, and says they are there to shape the future.

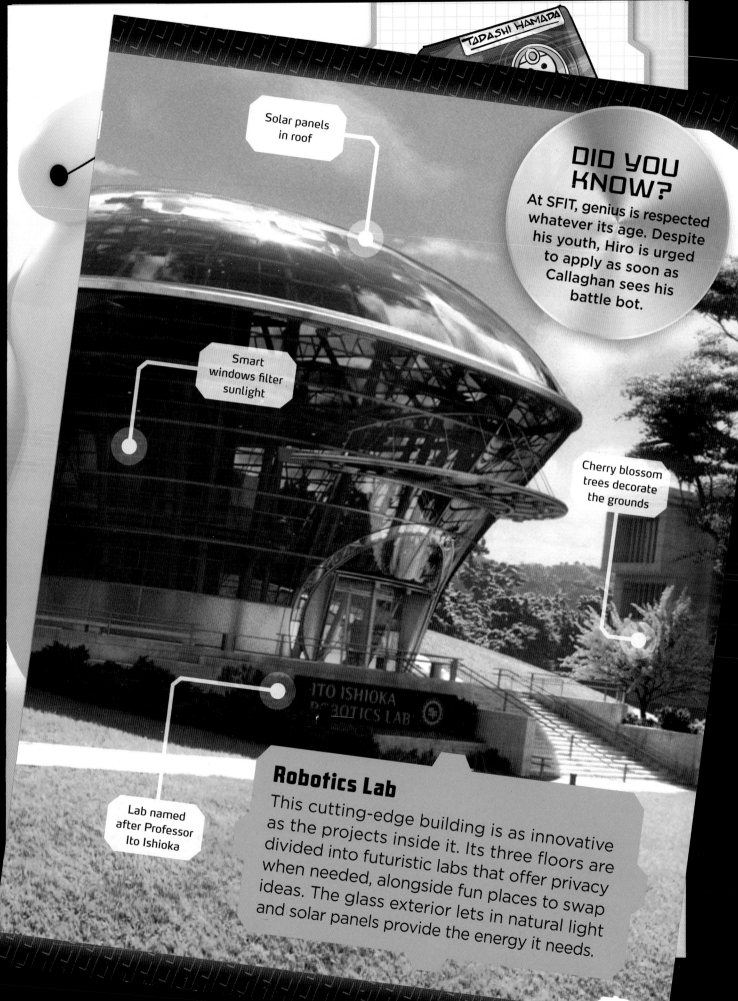

TADASHI HAMADA

Solar panels in roof

DID YOU KNOW?
At SFIT, genius is respected whatever its age. Despite his youth, Hiro is urged to apply as soon as Callaghan sees his battle bot.

Smart windows filter sunlight

Cherry blossom trees decorate the grounds

ITO ISHIOKA ROBOTICS LAB

Lab named after Professor Ito Ishioka

Robotics Lab

This cutting-edge building is as innovative as the projects inside it. Its three floors are divided into futuristic labs that offer privacy when needed, alongside fun places to swap ideas. The glass exterior lets in natural light and solar panels provide the energy it needs.

Go Go

Go Go combines a brilliant engineering mind with an insane love of extreme velocity. She likes building cutting-edge bikes with electro-magnetic suspension – then she usually recycles the wheels to make something even speedier!

Purple streak in hair shows punky attitude

Tadashi's team

Despite her tough, independent streak, Go Go is an integral member of Tadashi's team. She provides the cool attitude and the bold one-liners.

Tight clothes for less air resistance in motion

The quiet type

She may not be the chattiest character around, but when Go Go **does** speak, people listen. She has strong opinions about most things, which can annoy people, but her friends trust her instincts.

Wasabi

This super-organised nerd is a physics genius, but behind his swagger he is really very cautious and a neat-freak. However, he supports his pals to the max, even providing fresh underpants and breath mints at crucial moments.

Wasabi takes good care of his dreads

Hunky Wasabi favours figure-hugging jumpers

Everything in its place

Wasabi goes to incredible lengths to keep his work area pristine and in perfect order. There are even outlines on his desk to show exactly where each tool should go!

Big man on campus

Wasabi is a well-known figure at SFIT, with his powerful physique and big personality. His laser systems are so amazing that some students think he can invent anything – his friend Fred has asked for a laser to shrink himself with.

The Tech Showcase

Every year, San Fransokyo Tech prepares for a new influx of students with its traditional battle of the brains – the SFIT Tech Showcase. The event attracts VIPs of the science world, as well as stars of big business seeking to spot talent and steal a few ideas. Dreams become reality here, or end up shattered.

It's showtime!

Behind the bewildering array of mad inventions is a smoothly organised, serious event. Contenders are given strictly controlled booth-space to set up their project and put across their idea. The judges then offer the best candidates a coveted spot at SFIT.

Live digital displays

Hydrodynamic engineering display

DID YOU KNOW?

The showcase is a buzzing live show, where prospective students share technology that might just change the future.

28

4 Simple diagnost...

Lighting
highlights
entries

The Showcase Hall
One of the most exciting venues
at SFIT is the Showcase Hall.
Its imposing, traditional look
hides the explosion of creative
competition that goes on within.

Touchscreen
display panels

Main
walkway

Showcase
presentation
zone

> **"ON A SCALE OF ONE
> TO TEN, HOW WOULD
> YOU RATE YOUR PAIN?"**
>
> **—BAYMAX**

Bayma[x]

Hiro sinks into a life [...]
brother, Tadashi. He [...]
eating, not even both[...]
San Fransokyo Tech. [...]
unexpected form...

1 Hopping mad

Just when Hiro thinks his life can't get any worse he experiences the brief – but intense – agony of stubbing his toe. He grabs his sore foot, hops around, and cries out in pain.

Robotics books – untouched for weeks

2

se[...]
ce[...]
of [...]
Ta[...]
los[...]
Stu[...]
ca[...]
lea[...]
flo[...]

In no mood to be fussed over, Hiro tries to get Baymax to switch himself off again right away. He tells the robot he is fine – but Baymax isn't so sure. He scans his new patient and finds lots to worry about!

Baymax's Vision

This ever-friendly healthcare companion is a unique creation, and he sees the world in his own way. His hyperspectral camera eyes relay complicated data back to his computer brain, which projects the information onto an internal screen for him to study and make his diagnosis.

Hyperspectral cameras
Lenses pick up data invisible to the human eye, such as body heat and oxygen saturation of the blood.

DIAGNOSIS

MOOD SWINGS

LBG   RDC
006
005
004
003
002
001
000

SYMPTOMS

No Physical Injury
==================
Overactive Pituitary
High levels GnRH
High Testosterone

ECG
48
PACE .18
ST1 .52
ST2 .57
PVCs .55

Heart rate monitor

19.55 mmHg
113 90 80
Blood pressure levels

ECG readout
Analyses electrical signals in the heart in order to measure heart activity.

Blood pressure
Checks the pressure of blood circulating around the body.

Patient feedback display

Clear, user-friendly explanations of his medical analysis are absolutely vital for Baymax's patients. His vinyl body acts as a screen to display his findings. Relevant areas are highlighted in simple diagrams using soothing colours to prevent patient anxiety.

Neurological mapping
Electrical impulses in the brain are monitored to check senses and motion centers.

ADULT:

Typical adult brainwaves

SUBJECT:

Subject brainwaves

Alpha wave analysis

Brainwave data chart

Delta/theta comparison

Brain activity readouts
Data is compared in clear graphics for a fast check of all brain activity.

79	34	70	65	60	47

Continuous data log

Vital signs
Baymax can rapidly crunch numbers and work out Hiro's needs from complicated statistical analysis.

Microbot Attack!

After the fire at the Tech Showcase, Hiro never expects to see his microbots again – and he certainly doesn't expect to be attacked by an army of them! A shock find leads to a bizarre adventure with Baymax... who is really only trying to improve Hiro's health!

1 An unexpected discovery

Hiro trips over Baymax and falls onto his bedroom floor, where he notices something weird – the hoodie under his bed is vibrating. A microbot he left in its pocket wants to go somewhere...

"COME ON! LET'S GET OUT OF HERE! GO! HURRY!"

–HIRO

2 A robot about town

Hiro accidentally sends Baymax on a mission when he casually suggests he should find out where the microbot wants to go. Taking Hiro literally, Baymax obediently sets off across town with the microbot, as Hiro chases after him.

3 The warehouse

Baymax's quest takes him to an old, abandoned-looking warehouse. When Hiro catches up, he points out that the place is locked. Baymax, however, spots an open window – he has to deflate to squeeze through it!

4 Yokai!

When the determined pair get inside the warehouse, they discover a machine producing thousands of new microbots. This microbot army is under the control of a sinister masked figure. Under attack, Hiro and Baymax flee for their lives!

5 No help

The local police don't believe Hiro when he tells them that a man in a mask attacked him with an army of tiny robots! If Hiro wants to solve this mystery, he will have to do it on his own.

Yokai

This sinister super villain hides his identity behind a scary mask. Hiro realises that Yokai must have started the fire at the Tech Showcase and stolen his microbots, but why?
What is Yokai planning?
And most importantly, who is he?

Mask detaches from skullcap

Bulky outfit disguises body shape

Sinister purpose

At the Tech Showcase, Hiro bragged that his microbots had limitless uses. Now that they've fallen into the hands of this mysterious enemy, who knows what dark schemes he will use them for? One thing is certain – Yokai will try to crush anyone who gets in his way!

Masked menace

Yokai wears a traditional Japanese Noh theater mask. The red markings on its face are meant to symbolise anger.

Carbon fibre gloves

The new master

A neural transmitter in Yokai's mask enables him to control Hiro's microbots, forming them into a nasty array of deadly weapons and cunning traps.

DID YOU KNOW?

Yōkai is an ancient Japanese word meaning "ghost", or "bad guy".

Prepare for Battle

It's a shock for Hiro to discover that someone has stolen his tech and is building a microbot army. It's even worse when he realises that this enemy must have deliberately started the fire that killed Tadashi, in order to cover his tracks at the showcase. Hiro sets off on the dangerous path of revenge...

1 Upgrade time

Now that Hiro is determined to take on his sinister enemy, he needs serious back-up – it's time to upgrade Baymax. Hiro makes a new chip which gives Baymax some feisty karate moves. The gentle robot needs to toughen up, too, so Hiro builds him some mean armour.

2 Karate bot

it's time to try out Baymax's new fighting chip. Hiro has programmed the helpful bot to unleash the hammer fist, knife hand, side kick and back kick. In his new, non-cuddly armour Baymax can easily punch through a wooden board!

New carbon fibre armour

Hiro's garage serves as a training ground

3 Return to the warehouse

Hiro thinks they are all set for a showdown with their foe. They return to the villain's hideaway, and Baymax kicks the door open... but the warehouse is now empty. Hiro's microbot is now indicating that it wants to head elsewhere. The unwavering pair follow the jumpy microbot, as they close in on their target.

"OKAY BAYMAX, TIME TO USE THOSE UPGRADES."

−HIRO

Hiro takes cover before Baymax easily smashes the warehouse door down.

4 Down at the docks

The trail takes them down to the waterfront. Peering around a container they spot their enemy moving some strange equipment across the bay using the microbots. What is the masked menace up to? Before they can find out, Hiro's friends unexpectedly arrive. They were worried about Hiro, so they followed him, but their arrival means trouble...

Trouble at the Docks

Hiro leads his friends into trouble when he tries to solve the mystery of who is using his microbots. When he and Baymax track the enemy down to the docks, they are not expecting to be followed by Fred, Go Go, Wasabi and Honey. Soon the whole gang is in serious danger...

1 Chased by Yokai

Realising he is being spied on, Yokai launches an attack on the gang. Hiro wants to stay and fight, but after Yokai hurls a shipping container at them, his friends decide it's time to grab Hiro and get out of there. Yokai wants no witnesses and sets off in pursuit.

Baymax's added weight makes car hard to steer

Wasabi's small car is not an ideal getaway vehicle

Microbots can overcome any obstacle

bay

nics as
up with the
Go takes
ut Yokai
of
ath the
it upwards,
ramp into a
ne can see
going.They
speeding to
up
he bay!

3 No escape?

It looks like curtains for the gang as the car quickly starts to fill up with water, with them trapped inside! As it sinks to the bottom, Yokai watches, satisfied with his work.

4 Saved by Baymax

All is not lost... Baymax ditches his battered armour and reverts to his soft, huggable form. Inflating himself bigger than ever before, he rises upwards, lifting all the friends to the surface with him. Everyone is elated to be alive, but ever-focussed Baymax notes that they all have low temperatures and villain-related trauma.

HY ARE
RYING TO
US?!"

−WASABI

Baymax 2.0

After their first battle against Yokai ends badly, Hiro realises that Baymax will need a more serious upgrade. He gets some cool ideas from looking at Fred's collection of action figures. Soon Baymax 2.0 is the biggest action figure in town, but he still prefers healing people to fighting them.

ベイマックス

To the max

Hiro's battle bot-building skills come in handy when it comes to making Baymax more awesome. All he has to do is scale up. A 3-D printer makes his armour in no time!

TRUE OR FALSE?

Baymax's new thrusters are located in his legs.

TRUE: There isn't room for them anywhere else!

Upgraded hands can bend solid steel with ease

Power punch

On top of his karate skills, Baymax now has a spectacular new combat weapon – his rocket fists. Powered-up, they can blast off and smash holes in almost anything.

Lean mean flying machine

Baymax is air-bound with newly added thrusters combined with fold-out wings. It would be great if he also knew how to steer, but luckily Hiro is there to give him instructions.

Super sensor visor

Bird-design wings with metal feather sections

New armour protects against blast or impact damage

SUPER ABILITIES

- Flight power
- Rocket fists
- Super sensor
- Martial arts

Rocket fist slots into forearm

Thrusters built into leg sections

"FUNCTIONALITY IMPROVED. 1000% INCREASE IN RANGE."

Super Hiro

Hiro knows he and his friends will need to become much stronger before they try to defeat Yokai. Building Baymax 2.0 was just the start – Hiro is going to use his robotics skills to upgrade the rest of the gang, too, starting with himself!

TRUE OR FALSE?

Hiro's suit has electro-magnets inside it.

TRUE: He uses them to attach to Baymax.

Electro-magnetic gauntlets have built-in kevlar armour protection

Gadget pouch

Flying fighters
When Baymax goes into flying mode, Hiro locks onto him with his magnetic pads and gloves. This means the two can fly as one.

Electro-magnetically soled boots

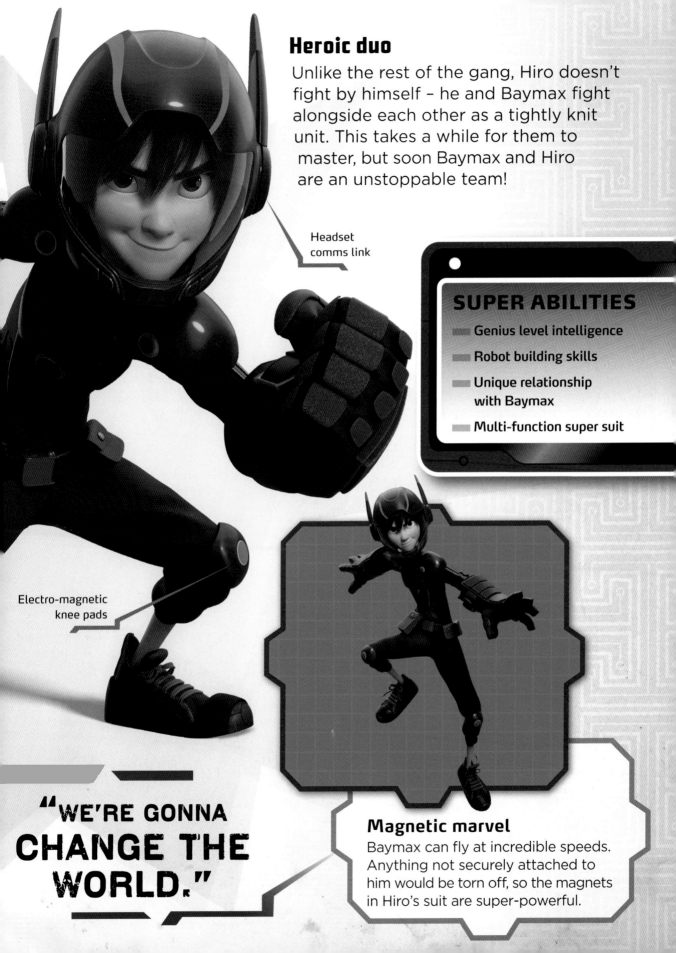

Heroic duo

Unlike the rest of the gang, Hiro doesn't fight by himself – he and Baymax fight alongside each other as a tightly knit unit. This takes a while for them to master, but soon Baymax and Hiro are an unstoppable team!

Headset comms link

SUPER ABILITIES

- Genius level intelligence
- Robot building skills
- Unique relationship with Baymax
- Multi-function super suit

Electro-magnetic knee pads

"WE'RE GONNA CHANGE THE WORLD."

Magnetic marvel

Baymax can fly at incredible speeds. Anything not securely attached to him would be torn off, so the magnets in Hiro's suit are super-powerful.

Super Go Go

A speed-freak before she even got a super suit, Go Go was born to be a super hero. After a few issues with balance at high velocity, she quickly masters her new gear and learns death-defying tricks. Fearless Go Go can't resist doing high-speed stunt jumps and roll-landings!

Gloves prevent friction burns

Speed wheels

Experiments with mag-lev (magnetic-levitation) technology have enabled Go Go to create frictionless wheels that are super-fast. The wheels also act as shields and throwing discs.

Jointed body-armour for crash protection

Detachable wheels held on by magnets

Aerodynamic fin controls airflow

Super slick

Go Go's suit is the most streamlined of all the team's costumes. It is designed to reduce drag and cut through the air. The unusual helmet is modelled after those used in Olympic speed-cycling events.

SUPER ABILITIES

- Super speed and agility
- Throwing discs that return magnetically
- At full speed, Go Go's mass creates a massive impact

Fast and Feisty

Go Go guides the team in key decisions. She's the first to tell Hiro that he won't be facing his enemy alone, and she is quick to keep Wasabi in line whenever he wavers. She also stands up to Hiro when his desire for revenge threatens to go too far.

TRUE OR FALSE?

Go Go's helmet is based on a fighter pilot's.

FALSE: It's based on a cyclist's!

51

Super Wasabi

Even though Wasabi is a powerful figure, he is still a bag of nerves when going into battle, and jumps at the occasional shadow. His deadly laser gloves mean he can defend himself from almost any attack, but he is frankly more worried about people messing with his stuff.

TRUE OR FALSE?
Wasabi wears a bandana to protect his head.

FALSE: He just wears it to look cool!

Armoured shoulder plates

Laser gloves
The super-hot plasma produced by Wasabi's gloves can form many differently shaped blades. These can slice through any known material with total ease.

Japanese boots known as *Jika-tabi* provide grip

ワサビ

"WE'RE NOT SUPER HEROES – WE'RE NERDS."

Superheated plasma

Smart visor filters out laser glare

Awesome armour

With samurai-style plated armour, Wasabi's suit is designed to afford him maximum protection from his own laser weapons. He wears a headset to link up with the rest of the team and a bandana just to look cool.

Warrior or worrier?

Wasabi is used to people expecting him to be tough and has learned to put on a fake swagger. The slightest unexpected danger, however, can freak him out. He is very methodical and always likes to have a working plan.

SUPER ABILITIES

- Physics genius
- Can generate laser blades
- Steel-cutting power
- Super organisational skills

53

Super Honey

Always upbeat, Honey becomes an unstoppable positive force when she goes into hero mode. Her eye-zapping costume reflects the energy and creativity she brings to the team, and her crazy array of chem-capsules can be just as surprising to her teammates as they are to her foes.

ハニーレモン

Potent purse

The strap of Honey's purse is a string of empty chem-capsules. These are passed into a micro chemical factory inside the bag, where syringes inject chemical cocktails into them. They are then released for use.

Chem-capsule interface shows chemical levels

TRUE OR FALSE?

Honey doesn't like dangerous situations.

FALSE: She loves them!

Addicted to danger

Honey seems to get a buzz from danger. Luckily her chemistry background makes her a whizz at mixing volatile substances to stunning effect. Among her chem-capsule weapons are a quick-freeze capsule, an instant net, and a tough plaster shield. She can also trap enemies in special sticky goo.

Long hair left untied, even in battle

SUPER ABILITIES

- Genius level chemistry skills
- Unique chem-capsule arsenal
- Advanced targeting system in helmet
- Super-accurate throwing

Advanced polyethylene shell

Light but lethal

Honey's costume is the least armoured of all the team's suits, in order to keep her light on her feet and swift in attack. The sleeves and leggings provide skin protection from chemical spillage.

Stylish wedges give added grip

"THAT WAS AMAZING!"

Super Fred

Fred makes a natural super hero – he actually thinks being attacked by super villains is cool. He is now living his dream and can't help speaking in a corny monologue just like a real comic book character. Although a soft-hearted dude, Fred is in touch with his inner monster.

Flame effect arm fins

Inside the monster
Fred's suit conceals a sophisticated flame-thrower, mounted just below his chest. The suit's feet have built-in pogo-bounce tech.

The Beast
Fred loves Japanese monster movies, and the design of his costume is meant to terrify. With horns, fins, claws and more, it may seem cumbersome, but Fred wears so-called Kaiju monster suits for fun. He is completely at home in one.

Eye lens gives night vision

"IT'S FRED TIME!"

SUPER ABILITIES
- Super-jump
- Breathing fire (of all kinds)
- Smokescreen
- Sign spinning

Flames hot enough to melt steel

TRUE OR FALSE?
Fred's suit allows him to jump to great heights.

TRUE: Fred loves to super-jump into battle!

Carbon fibre claws provide extra grip

Burning sensation
Fred has complete control over his flame-thrower, enabling him to pick the right heat for any situation. Supernova, fireball and flame-grilled are just some of the options.

Krei's mistake
During the critical test mission into the portal, technicians report an irregularity in the field harmonics. Krei thinks it is within acceptable parameters, and goes ahead with the ill-fated mission anyway.

Warning lights indicate portal is activated

DID YOU KNOW?
The sparrow is a symbol of unexpected fortune in Japanese folklore, and a reward for kindness.

Maintenance ramp for portal

One-pilot flight pod

Akuma Island

Just offshore of San Fransokyo bay is a secret test facility belonging to Krei Tech. Here, billions of dollars have been poured into Alistair Krei's "Project Silent Sparrow". It aims to achieve a scientific dream: teleportation.

Project Silent Sparrow

The technology behind this incredible experiment is housed in a vast chamber hidden away from all but a privileged few. Twin portals are powered up to open a path into an unknown dimension. But the technology is untested, and disaster looms...

Teleport field generated by inner ring

Landing zone to catch pod exiting portal

Intrepid pilot

The brave figure in the flight pod is Krei's test pilot. Krei has told her loved ones that the portal technology is safe, but no one truly knows what will happen.

Go Team!

The gang may have the tech skills to turn themselves into super heroes, but now they must prove they really have what it takes to battle a bad guy. Thanks to Baymax's super sensor they have tracked their enemy, Yokai, down to the portal lab on Akuma Island. There's no turning back now.

Battle in the portal lab

The intrepid gang arrives to find that the lab on Akuma Island has been totally destroyed. Project Silent Sparrow went badly wrong, and the test pilot was lost inside the portal! Yokai ambushes Hiro and his friends, but the heroic team surprise their foe by fighting back with their new powers. Hiro manages to knock Yokai's mask off, but the villain gets away with the last pieces of the portal.

Laser blades deflect microbot attack

Friendly fire

Go Go zooms in to battle Yokai, but she skids on a patch of ice created by one of Honey's chem-capsules. These individuals will have to learn the art of teamwork!

"We didn't set out to be super heroes. But sometimes life doesn't go the way you planned. The good thing is my brother wanted to help a lot of people. And that's what we're going to do. Who are we?...

Honey

Fred

Wasabi

Go Go

Hiro

Baymax

...We are
Big Hero 6!"

Acknowledgements

Penguin Random House

Editor David Fentiman
Senior Designer Lisa Robb
Design by Mark Richards, Lisa Robb, Toby Truphet
Pre-Production Producer Siu Yin Chan
Senior Producer Alex Bell
Managing Editor Laura Gilbert
Managing Art Editor Maxine Pedliham
Art Director Lisa Lanzarini
Publisher Julie Ferris
Publishing Director Simon Beecroft

Published in Great Britain
in 2015 by Dorling Kindersley Limited
80 Strand, London, WC2R 0RL

10 9 8 7 6 5 4 3 2 1
001–255726–Jan/15

Page design copyright © 2015 Dorling Kindersley Limited
A Penguin Random House Company

A CIP catalogue record for this book is available
from the British Library.

ISBN 978-1-40934-932-7

Colour reproduction by Altaimage, UK
Printed and bound in the Slovak Republic by TBB, a.s.

DK would like to thank Danny Saeva, Heather Knowles,
Maria Elena Naggi, Winnie Ho, and Chelsea Alon at Disney Publishing,
Renato Lattanzi at Disney Consumer Products, and Roy Conli,
Lauren Brown, Albert Ramirez, and Andy Sinur at
Disney Animation Studios.

A WORLD OF IDEAS:
SEE ALL THERE IS TO KNOW